HEAVENLY
VISITATION 2

Unless otherwise indicated, Scripture quotations are taken from the New King James Version. Copyright © 1982 by Thomas Nelson, Inc. Used by permission. All rights reserved.

Scripture quotations marked (AMP) are taken from the Amplified Bible, Copyright © 1954, 1958, 1962, 1964, 1965, 1987 by The Lockman Foundation. Used by permission. www.Lockman.org. (The AMP regularly uses parentheses and brackets throughout. Unless otherwise noted, these are in the original and were not added by the author.)

Scripture quotations marked (ESV) are from the ESV® Bible (The Holy Bible, English Standard Version®), copyright © 2001 by Crossway, a publishing ministry of Good News Publishers. Used by permission. All rights reserved.

All Scripture quotations marked (KJV) are taken from the King James Version. Public Domain.

Scripture quotations marked (NIV) are taken from the Holy Bible, New International Version®, NIV®. Copyright © 1973, 1978, 1984, 2011 by Biblica, Inc.™ Used by permission of Zondervan. All rights reserved worldwide. www.zondervan.com The "NIV" and "New International Version" are trademarks registered in the United States Patent and Trademark Office by Biblica, Inc.™

Scripture quotations marked (NLT) are taken from the Holy Bible, New Living Translation, copyright ©1996, 2004, 2015 by Tyndale House Foundation. Used by permission of Tyndale House Publishers, a Division of Tyndale House Ministries, Carol Stream, Illinois 60188. All rights reserved.

Scripture quotations marked (TPT) are from The Passion Translation®. Copyright © 2017, 2018 by Passion & Fire Ministries, Inc. Used by permission. All rights reserved. www.thePassionTranslation.com.

Please note that Warrior Notes publishing style capitalizes certain pronouns in Scripture that refer to the Father, Son, and Holy Spirit, which may differ from some publishers' styles. Take note that the name "satan" and related names are not capitalized. We choose not to acknowledge him, even to the point of violating accepted grammatical rules. The author and Warrior Notes have made an intentional decision to italicize many Scriptures in block quotes. The italics are not intended to indicate emphasis unless otherwise noted.

Warrior Notes Publishing

P O Box 1288

Destrehan, LA 70047

Cover design: Virtually Possible Designs

For more information about our school, go to www.warriornotesschool.com.
Reach us on the internet: www.kevinzadai.com

ISBN 13 TP: 978-1-6631-0200-3

ISBN 13 eBook: 978-1-6631-0202-7

ISBN 13 Audiobook: 978-1-6631-0201-0

Dedication

I dedicate this book to the Lord Jesus Christ. When I died during surgery and met with Jesus on the other side, He insisted that I return to life on earth and help people with their destinies. Because of Jesus's love and concern for people, the Lord has actually chosen to send a person back from death to help everyone who will receive that help so that their destiny and purpose are secure in Him.

I want You, Lord, to know that when You come to take me to be with You someday, I sincerely hope that people remember not me but the revelation of Jesus Christ through me. I want others to know that I am merely being obedient to my heavenly calling and mission, which is to reveal Your plan to fulfill the divine destiny for each of God's children.

Acknowledgments

I n addition to sharing my story with everyone through the book *Heavenly Visitation: A Guide to the Supernatural*, God has commissioned me to write over eighty books and study guides. Most recently, the Lord gave me the commission to produce this book, *Heavenly Visitation 2*. This book addresses some of the revelations concerning the areas that Jesus showed me through the Word of God and by the Spirit of God during several visitations. I want to thank everyone who has encouraged, assisted, and prayed for me while writing this work. Special thanks to my wonderful wife, Kathi, for her love and dedication to the Lord and me. Thank you to my excellent staff for the beautiful job editing this book.

Contents

Revelation of the Future

J esus showed me many revelations about this realm (the future) that I want to share with you throughout this book. Some of what I was shown is complex and even controversial at times, and satan has resisted these spiritual truths. He does not want you to know and understand God's perfect will for your life.

Being in Heaven gave me a whole different perspective because I saw that eternal life from a heavenly perspective is so much more effective. It is more real, vaster than earth, and lasts forever. This world is just broken and slow, and so much disappointment is down here; it's hard to live here at times. As I was with Jesus, I saw the discrepancy between these two worlds.

In Heaven, I was given a revelation of the future and how God needs us to agree with His will. He has a plan for the earth, and our agreement will impact what is accomplished in support of God's kingdom. This was shocking to me, but as I've studied the Word over the many years since my heavenly visitation, I now see it.

*For I know the thoughts that I think toward you, saith the
LORD, thoughts of peace, and not of evil, to give you an
expected end.*

—Jeremiah 29:11 KJV

In Heaven, I saw that He has an expected end for us as the previous
verse tells us. I saw that God has plans that are perfect, wonderful plans
beyond what we can ask or think (Ephesians 3:20). Jeremiah wrote
this, and interestingly, he also wrote about Israel and Jerusalem and
how God's plan has always been for Israel to prosper. In Heaven, Jesus
showed me that He does not want many terrible things that happen,
but He permits them.

When you look at the borders of Israel given in Genesis 15, they
encompass almost the whole Middle East in comparison to the borders
that exist today (Genesis 15:18–21). God's will, His perfect will, has
not been fulfilled. Although the nation of Israel exists, it's approxi-
mately the size of New Jersey, which is a small state compared to other
American states. The biblical borders account for most of the Middle
East, from Egypt all the way across to Iran, all the northern territories,
and Turkey. In this plan, Israel would own all the oil in the Middle East.

The authority given to us as the church is a great responsibility that
I don't think is being recognized. The Spirit of God wants to show us
God's intentions. He wants us to bind and loose and secure the position
through agreement, prayer, and intercession. Christians must do this to
allow God's plan to flourish in our lives, as well as in our communities
and the church. Otherwise, His plans will be delayed, and we will allow
the enemy's plans to come to fruition.

We see terrible things that happen that are not God's will. It's conditional, like when Paul told Timothy, "This is why I remind you to

fan into flames the spiritual gift God gave you when I laid my hands on you" (2 Timothy 1:6 NLT). When Paul laid hands on Timothy, there were flames on him, but they had turned to coals. In this verse, Paul was giving the responsibility back to Timothy to take a proactive step. Earlier, in 1 Timothy 1:18, Paul counseled Timothy to wage war with the prophecies he had received that had not come to pass. He wanted Timothy to use prophecies as weapons of war. Your future and the revelation of it have more to do with your engagement in God's will. It's going to take faith manifested through your words and actions.

I was recently praying and seeking an answer about the future. I needed direction about what to do in the final few months of the year. I was surprised when the Lord answered. "I want you to come out with Heavenly Visitation 2 and share on these other subjects that you did not include in the first book." It caught me by surprise, but the Lord showed me that it is like a time capsule, and He wants certain information to be released at a specific time.

I knew in the back of my mind that I would probably write more about what Jesus taught me. When I was in Heaven with the Lord, He sent me back with so much information, it felt like years' worth of truths.

> I will give you the keys (authority) of the kingdom of heaven; and whatever you bind [forbid, declare to be improper and unlawful] on earth will have [already] been bound in heaven, and whatever you loose [permit, declare lawful] on earth will have [already] been loosed in heaven.

> —Matthew 16:19 AMP

I have written this book to share that we need to be responsible and take accountability. We have been given keys to God's kingdom, and we have the authority to bind on earth and loose in Heaven, which is the forbidding and permitting of God's will. Finally, if we agree as touching any one thing, it shall be done for us (Matthew 18:19). God wants the glorious church to have the last say in all matters on earth.

Chapter 1

Prophetic Scenarios

And you will hear of wars and threats of wars, but don't panic. Yes, these things must take place, but the end won't follow immediately. Nation will go to war against nation, and kingdom against kingdom. There will be famines and earthquakes in many parts of the world. But all this is only the first of the birth pains, with more to come.

—Matthew 24:6–8 NLT

Many people are focused on current events and want to know where we are in the Bible's prophetic timeline. However, much of what is happening in the world is the birth pangs that Jesus told us about here in the Gospel of Matthew. It's just the beginning, and what we see happening in the world does not necessarily place us in the end times.

Occasionally, we can pinpoint biblical prophecies within our current events; however, I want to emphasize in this book how to figure out what the Lord is saying to you individually, your fellowship group, your church, and the state or country that you live in. You have the same ability to hear God as every other believer. You do not need to wait to be told by a person in the fivefold ministry to know prophetically what God is saying to you.

> *I must go on boasting. Although there is nothing to be gained, I will go on to visions and revelations from the Lord. I know a man in Christ who fourteen years ago was caught up to the third heaven. Whether it was in the body or out of the body I do not know—God knows. And I know that this man—whether in the body or apart from the body I do not know, but God knows— was caught up to paradise and heard inexpressible things, things that no one is permitted to tell. I will boast about a man like that, but I will not boast about myself, except about my weaknesses.*

—2 Corinthians 12:1–5 NIV

Here in 2 Corinthians, Paul is talking about his own experience of being caught up with the Lord. He is explaining to people where his insight and authority came from—it was imparted to him by Jesus Christ.

When Paul was first converted, he went away to Arabia for a time, probably close to three years (Galatians 1:17). Many believe that he was caught up during this timeframe, most likely on Mount Sinai, and Jesus directly taught him the gospel.

Obviously, these experiences are not common to every believer, but we see many of the apostles and prophets experiencing supernatural events. God wants to speak to you personally, and He has many ways to do so. God creates prophetic scenarios for each generation that can be interpreted by the Spirit. People assume that God is speaking a certain thing, but He may be saying something completely different. It's important that we stay in the Word of God, especially right now and in the days ahead.

EVERY VOICE MUST DECLARE GOD'S WORD

I want to emphasize these two points:

1. You can create an environment where you can hear from God and have revelation regarding your county and region.

2. You can speak out what God reveals to you and prophesy, and your prophetic voice will activate God's will.

God has given you a platform, so whatever that platform is, you must use it to speak prophetically, no matter what your function. I believe that everyone should prophesy; you must speak the Word of God. You are equipped to speak to mountains, but also, in these last days, you are called to speak to current and future environments.

The foundation of prophecy is the Word of God, and it must be filled with the Spirit of God. Prior to every conference, filming a course for Warrior Notes School of Ministry, or writing a book, I gather and meditate on upwards of one hundred Scriptures. This is the foundation for ministry, and it must be your foundation as a prophetic mouthpiece of the Lord.

> *In those days I will pour out my Spirit even on my servants—men and women alike—and they will prophesy.*

> —Acts 2:18 NLT

God is pouring out His Spirit in these days, and His servants will prophesy. To prophesy what the Spirit is saying, it is helpful to increase your vocabulary and understanding of the Word of God. It's time to become well-versed in different subjects in the Bible and expand your knowledge and comprehension. I have noticed that since I started increasing my studies, especially in these last fifteen years, my ability to prophesy has increased because of the connection I have with the Word of God. Once the Word is within me, the Spirit can grab those words and principles and use those in prophecy.

So, when I teach, it's prophetic. When I speak the Word of God and pray, all the power of the Spirit of God is available. This comes because I have established myself in the knowledge of the Scriptures. God's people received the Scriptures in the Old Testament, and then during the New Testament, in the time of the early church, men and women were moved by the Holy Spirit, and they wrote the Scriptures.

Of course, we know that today, apostles and prophets are no longer writing Scripture. God appointed a certain time for that, for the foundation to be laid. Now, the written Word of God is complete, and we have everything that we need. Even though much more could have been shared, you remember when John said. "Jesus also did many other things. If they were all written down, I suppose the whole world could not contain the books that would be written" (John 21:25 NLT).

We only have a portion of what was said and what was done. However, it is sufficient, and the Spirit of God will help us fill in the pieces. Scripture has been breathed out by God, inspired by the Holy Spirit, and it is for teaching (2 Timothy 3:16–17).

You may not feel as though you have the gift of teaching, but those gifts can be developed. I didn't necessarily think that I had a gift initially.

I have developed that over the last thirty years. I've been saved for close to forty-five years, and my teaching gift has especially increased and developed over the past ten years. The gift was probably inside me all along, but it only came out after lots of studying and teaching—and believe me, I do a lot of teaching!

THE PROFITABILITY OF THE WORD

All Scripture is given by inspiration of God, and is profitable for doctrine, for reproof, for correction, for instruction in righteousness.

—2 Timothy 3:16

Teaching: Doctrine

The Word is profitable for *teaching*, but everyone should learn to do a Bible study and teach. I believe that we are all called to that. You do not have to be an extravagant or charismatic figure who can stand in front of a large crowd. You should be able to communicate and develop your skills to distribute the gospel effectively. Everyone in the body, especially pastors, should be able to teach on some level.

Reproof

All Scripture is also profitable for *reproof*, which means to confirm and bring evidence. I always have two or three Scriptures for everything I am teaching. If I can't find two or three Scriptures, then I just express what I feel (my opinion). But you won't hear me say that too often because I stay away from conjecture. I want to obtain proof and then reproof that. Reproof brings confirmation or will bring down false doctrines.

Correction

Correction is another important function of the Word. Paul also does this many times in his letters. In referring to habitual, sinful lifestyles, Paul told the Corinthians, "Let me tell you again, as I have before, that anyone living that sort of life will not inherit the kingdom of God" (Galatians 5:21 NLT). He reminded them by saying he had told them this before. Paul was often very adamant when he wrote about corrective measures. Here is an example of Paul telling Timothy about the state of men in the last days.

> *For people will love only themselves and their money. They will be boastful and proud, scoffing at God, disobedient to their parents, and ungrateful. They will consider nothing sacred. They will be unloving and unforgiving; they will slander others and have no self-control. They will be cruel and hate what is good. They will betray their friends, be reckless, be puffed up with pride, and love pleasure rather than God. They will act religious, but they will reject the power that could make them godly. Stay away from people like that!*
>
> —2 Timothy 3:2–5 NLT

Training: Instruction

Lastly, Paul describes Scripture as being good for *training in righteousness*. Many people do not understand that when you speak, teach, and minister prophetically by the Spirit, you must also lay forth the foundation of righteousness; you want to bring God's justice into the situation.

That is the prophetic scenario for these days. The world is off, and the spirit of the world is working in this time. It has infiltrated the church as we see Jesus reveal it to John in the book of Revelation (Revelation 2–3). We are to train and follow the path of righteousness, which brings justice. The righteous path brings deliverance, healing, and correction.

TRUTH IS A FOUNDATION

> *Jesus said to him, "I am the [only] Way [to God] and the [real] Truth and the [real] Life; no one comes to the Father but through Me."*

> —John 14:6 AMP

Jesus told us that He is the way, the truth, and the life and that no one goes to the Father but through Him. This is the foundation and basis—He is the truth. We must focus on this foundation and look at the Spirit of God as the person who is going to lead us into all that truth (John 16:13).

THE SPIRIT RESPONDS TO HIS VOICE

The earth was without form, and void; and darkness was on the face of the deep. And the Spirit of God was hovering over the face of the waters. Then God said, "Let there be light"; and there was light.

—Genesis 1:2–3

When God spoke, the Spirit was right there to form and separate light from darkness, and the days of creation began. The spirit of prophecy wants to come upon you and cause you to speak. I have had the spirit of prophecy come upon me while I was at work, and I would prophesy to people who weren't even saved. I have had the Spirit of God come on me in prayer meetings or when I have been out talking to people; suddenly, the word of the Lord would come to me, and I would prophesy.

The Spirit of God is not restricted to a church service. He can move at any time, in any place. At times, I've even woken up in the middle of the night, prophesying out loud to myself and my wife, Kathi. The Spirit of God has come upon us, and we've been shown prophetic scenarios. This happens to me often, both during the day and at night.

The Spirit shows me visions, flashes, and glimpses of the future and of situations that are happening right now. My dreams show me trouble spots, current and pending events. One experience that sticks out to me is a time when I was in a deep sleep at night, and I saw the return of the Lord, the saints, and the horses. Jesus was on His horse, wearing a huge gold crown with gemstones in it. He had light beams coming out of His eyes. Jesus looked at me, and I saw the angels and the saints with Him in the clouds, and He was coming.

When He looked my way, the light beams hit me, and I started to rejoice and worship Him. Kathi, who was also in a deep sleep, began worshiping Him as well. She was seeing the same things, and the light beams hit her too. He looked at us, and then we both woke up. This was an amazing visitation that we had together, and we saw the same thing.

In the days ahead, God wants to show you things and give you scenarios, give you His plan for every situation. Many times, we look at the news and see events that are happening, such as natural disasters. But see, Jesus said that these signs were just the beginning. These types of events weren't signs of the end. The end had not come yet. He tells us that earthquakes and disasters are just birth pangs.

In the end, we will begin to have signs in the heavens. Deception will happen, and we're going to see the other realms coming into this one. Demonic forces will begin to reveal themselves in the skies above and come out of the ground. We will see these types of signs coming. I want to encourage you to stay grounded in the Word of God. When these disasters come, don't try to interpret them because they are just part of the scenario at the end and part of the birth pangs.

You must pray in the Spirit, study the Word of God, and allow God to show you the prophetic scenarios that are for you, your territory, and your platform. Wherever it is that God has placed you, He wants you to speak. He wants you to speak against anything that is happening that is of the enemy. God wants you to speak into existence the things on the other side. Through agreeing in prayer and prophesying, we can bring forth God's plan.

When God warns me about what is coming, I step in and stop the situation. I pray against them. God shows me His perfect will. It may be the person He wants in leadership or the direction He wants a country to go, different situations like that. But it is up to me to pray so the enemy cannot have his way. You must see that God gives us templates—prophetic scenarios that He is laying out for us to follow. He is also exposing what satan is doing so that we can pray and prophesy against the enemy's plan.

Chapter 2

Dreams and Visions

For God may speak in one way, or in another, yet man does not perceive it. In a dream, in a vision of the night, when deep sleep falls upon men, while slumbering on their beds, then He opens the ears of men, and seals their instruction. In order to turn man from his deed, and conceal pride from man.

—Job 33:14–17

I n this chapter, I want to examine different types of visions that the Lord gives and differentiate between them. The Spirit operates in varying degrees for different people, so I will share from my own experiences as well as from the Scriptures.

We must understand that we have the other realm inside us, the spiritual realm. We can access this and know situations ahead of time. As a result of the Spirit within us, we can see into this timeless realm where there is no distance and no time has passed even between points in time.

Basically, in the timeless realm, there is no real time in travel, and it doesn't matter how far the distance is when there is an absence of time.

There are no reference points for this, and you can travel instantly in this realm.

When I was with Jesus for forty-five minutes during my heavenly visitation, it was just like the book of Revelation was occurring. I could see events happening in an instant, but it was also futuristic. Some events were in the past, but He would just raise his hand slightly and beckon the destination to come to Him. We never went; the location was brought to us. I never moved, and yet we were there. There was no distance because the destinations would obey Him and come. Past, present and future, He commanded them all.

This is why you must believe that you receive before you have it (Mark 11:24). Think of it this way: God is not limited by the fallen earth, and He can work through us. He is only limited by whether man uses the authority he's been given.

The keys have been given to the church. God has given us all authority, authority to bind and loose. If we don't loose something, then it stays bound. If something is loose, then we must verbally bind it. God then agrees with that. If we don't agree as touching something, it won't be done, and if we believe we receive it, it really comes to us. We don't go to it and see.

Faith is the substance of things hoped for (Hebrews 11:1). We have it. It's the evidence of things not seen. You have evidence of it before you get it because it actually exists. It's in another realm, but it is truly obtainable.

We tend to think of faith as like a lever we pull. However, faith is a trust and a relationship that we have with God where we operate at a higher level and therefore receive what has not yet happened on this earth. God allows us to receive ahead of time through faith.

Now after six days Jesus took Peter, James, and John his brother, led them up on a high mountain by themselves; and He was transfigured before them. His face shone like the sun, and His clothes became as white as the light. And behold, Moses and Elijah appeared to them, talking with Him.

—Matthew 17:1–3

On the Isle of Patmos, John saw the end time scenario, but he didn't just see a movie. He was literally there. This event hasn't occurred on earth yet. Similarly, when Jesus was on the Mount of Transfiguration, Peter, James and John were there with Him and Moses.

When Moses was on the mountain with Jesus getting the law, Elijah appeared there before he even existed. Peter, James, and John saw the meeting that had already happened. Elijah was taken back from the future to that point, and they all observed that. But actually, it was all occurring in a timeless realm.

When I pray, I know I've got what I prayed for; otherwise, I wouldn't pray. How did I learn that? Through trust. I didn't learn it through building up some sort of system we call faith. It isn't a system. We are connecting with God on an intimate level, which means we become one with Him in spirit. We have the ability to speak and change things through prayer. We speak to mountains, but we don't see the mountains removed because we don't understand the fact that we are operating at a higher level in a different dimension and realm.

GLIMPSES OF THE FUTURE

This isn't new age—God wants to give us snapshots. He gives us glimpses of the future to help us understand where we're going, which is one purpose of dreams. The other purpose of dreams is to show the spiritual atmosphere, whether good or bad.

A lot of errors surround the topic of the supernatural, which prompted me to write about this subject. It's good to desire and have all these experiences with the Lord. After all, Christianity is an experience. It can be knowledge and understanding, but it is also the application of what we learn as we follow God and study His Word. In other words, God works with us, and part of it is that we encounter Him. He's a living God, right? So we should expect to have experiences, but we must stay within the Word of God because some experiences that people have are not correct and contradict the Word.

> *Beloved, do not believe every spirit, but test the spirits, whether they are of God; because many false prophets have gone out into the world.*
>
> —1 John 4:1

It is up to each individual to know the Word and weigh circumstances and experiences against that knowledge. This verse in 1 John is a warning. Overall, the body of Christ is not where it should be and is lacking in sensitivity to the truth. We must do better and help people mature. When Paul addressed the church in Corinth in 1 Corinthians 12 and 14, he gave them parameters and boundaries for what should and shouldn't happen when believers gather together.

The Spirit was moving, and people were interrupting each other and saying things that weren't of the Spirit. So Paul was laying a foundation for church order and communicating that the Holy Spirit does not operate in a chaotic way.

In 1 Corinthians 14:29, Paul tells the Corinthian church members that when someone is exercising a gift, they should judge what is being said. This is interesting, and it makes me wonder what would change if we were more accountable to one another.

With prophecy, we must understand that we know in part, and we speak in part (1 Corinthians 13:9). We do not fully participate in the revelations of God. At times, the Holy Spirit shows us something that we don't understand. Some prophetic scenarios that we see may be conditional. The Holy Spirit is revealing God's will, but we have to fight and wage war with them, just like Paul told Timothy to wage war with the prophecy that he had received, as I mentioned earlier (1 Timothy 1:18). As a teacher, I want to ensure that everyone in the body of Christ is operating at the highest level because we need to hear from God to be encouraged.

VISIONS OF GOD'S WILL

God often gives visions about matters that are still pending. He either shows us what His perfect will is, or we see the outcome that will occur if we don't make a change. These visions are conditional, and they show us God's intention.

A vision could be at night, during the day, or just a flash or a mental image. God often shows me open visions. When this happens, I will be going about my day, and suddenly, everything will disappear in front of me.

In 1993, right before Kathi and I were married, we had stopped to eat lunch in eastern Washington at a fast-food restaurant called Taco

Time. When we got there, I went to the restroom, and when I walked in, immediately, the whole restroom was gone. I was physically still there, but the whole wall disappeared, and Jesus was standing there. He visited with me just for thirty–forty seconds. During this vision, Jesus spoke to me about my marriage to Kathi and gave me guidance, all of which came to pass. After He gave me the word, the vision ended, and I could see the restroom again. We ate lunch and then left, and I later shared the vision with Kathi.

There are also quick flashes and glimpses, where you see a flash of God's will and He shows you information, knowledge, and wisdom. In these types of visions, your natural faculties are suspended. That is what is happening in an open vision—you are completely suspended.

Another example was when I lived in Phoenix. I had a four-mile track that I ran on through the desert, and sometimes, I would run it more than once. When you're running, you breathe hard, and you are maintaining your pace. In Arizona, you are also dealing with the intense heat and managing accordingly. So you get the idea; a lot is going on. While on this run, suddenly, I walked into a vision.

I was in a field. I could hear my labored breathing and my footsteps, and I didn't understand it, but I was still running straight on the path. As I entered the vision, I walked out to Jesus and talked with Him for about a minute. He was dressed as a warrior and clothed in red and blue garments. His breastplate was gold, and He had a large sword. That was the first revelation I had of God as a warrior and also of Zephaniah 3:17, which is the Scripture that Warrior Notes was founded on.

> *The LORD your God is in your midst, A Warrior who saves.*
> *He will rejoice over you with joy; He will be quiet in His*

love [making no mention of your past sins], He will rejoice over you with shouts of joy.

—Zephaniah 3:17 AMP

In the vision, Jesus spoke to me concerning a situation I was in at the time. I had been doubting my decision, and He encouraged me and explained that I had done the right thing. We make many decisions in life, and we all need encouragement at times. This happens to me often. God will confirm in a flash or a full vision. When He finished talking, I came out of the vision and could see the path. I had run quite a distance without even knowing or being aware of what I was doing. It was just amazing.

VISIONS OF THE NIGHT

And it shall come to pass afterward That I will pour out My Spirit on all flesh; Your sons and your daughters shall prophesy, Your old men shall dream dreams, Your young men shall see visions.

—Joel 2:28

At times, in the night, you may be sleeping, or you may even be taken in the Spirit, and it will be real. You may have vivid and more realistic dreams, which are night visions. These are different than a dream. I've had visitations of Jesus, which lasted part of the night. One night vision I had lasted about five hours. I was taken away to a building where Jesus spoke to me about Warrior Notes and the various departments. He walked me through each step, showed me intricate details about the ministry, and gave me many warnings.

I sat and listened to Jesus and never said a word. I was never given any time to say anything to Him. He spoke and addressed every area of the ministry while I listened. He told me about what was to come, the hardships that the ministry would face, and the hardships that would come to the United States. He explained to me the importance of what Warrior Notes would be doing to prepare people for the future. God wants us to have a clear vision, and He wants us to make it plain and write it down (Habakkuk 2:2). That is why the vision Jesus shared with me became the book *The Vision and Battle Strategy of Warrior Notes Ministries.*

DREAMS AND INTERPRETATIONS

Unlike visions, which are glimpses and flashes of God's will, dreams are more symbolic, and they can be confusing. Dreams can be a clue into a person's soul realm—their mind, will, and emotions. When you are unconscious and you have a dream, your subconscious will generate images from your psychological makeup, which are not necessarily generated by the Spirit of God. You may be tempted to begin interpreting from the soul realm. I want to caution you that dreams are symbolic, and you want to focus on interpreting dreams based on prayer and the Word of God to help you sort through the origin of your dreams.

If you have a dream and you don't understand the symbolism, just remember that if God gave you that dream, He wants you to understand it as well. There are some books and resources on symbology, but don't rely too heavily on those resources since the symbols in your dreams might be just for you. Begin by asking why a symbol or object was used in the dream because it may mean something to you personally and might not be something you can find in a book.

You don't need to interpret many general symbols too deeply. Many dreams warn about present situations. When you are operating in the prophetic, you must remember that your dreams will be impacted by the spiritual atmosphere of where you live. When I travel to different cities, I also experience different dreams that are influenced by the atmosphere and by which demonic entities preside over the area.

Your spirit will be able to see what is going on in the spiritual realm, but when your subconscious attempts to decipher this, it will not always translate properly. This is because we are not fully developed and transformed in the renewal of our minds (Romans 12:2).

I have found that when I constantly feed on the Word of God and keep myself from any evil in what I see and hear, my soul is not full of junk, and my dreams are pure. If I see or hear scary things in movies or in the news, then they will leave an impression on me, and my soul will influence my dreams. So you must understand that not every dream is God telling you something. Some dreams are prompted by the spiritual environment around you.

Dreams are very valuable. They show you what the enemy is up to. Dreams give you insight into what is happening behind the scenes as God warns you about spiritual wickedness. I deal with this by going to prayer and canceling anything negative I see.

At times, I have had recurring dreams about something happening to me, and so I will come against what I see and break it in the Spirit, and it will not come to fruition. At times in the past, I have ignored the warning and regretted it because what I saw came to pass.

You must always have the Word of God before you. Then, as you renew your mind, over the years, your dreams will be cleaned up and become purer to the point where you operate in a greater measure of the prophetic.

Chapter 3

Revelation of the Now: Word of Knowledge

There are diversities of gifts, but the same Spirit. There are differences of ministries, but the same Lord. And there are diversities of activities, but it is the same God who works all in all. But the manifestation of the Spirit is given to each one for the profit of all: for to one is given the word of wisdom through the Spirit, to another the word of knowledge through the same Spirit.

—1 Corinthians 12:4–8

The term *revelation of the now* can also be understood as the word of knowledge, which Paul lists in 1 Corinthians as one of the gifts of the Spirit. This is not to be confused with the word of wisdom, which we will talk about in the next chapter.

We are all called, and we all have gifts. The fivefold members of the body are chosen exclusively by God and then set in the church by Him. Paul said he was chosen to be an apostle from birth (Romans 1:1;

Galatians 1:15). That's early, isn't it? It seems surprising, especially since he spent half his life killing Christians and working against God. We know that even though that gift was there, it wasn't realized, and Paul wasn't walking in his gifting.

> *And [His gifts to the church were varied and] He Himself appointed some as apostles [special messengers, representatives], some as prophets [who speak a new message from God to the people], some as evangelists [who spread the good news of salvation], and some as pastors and teachers [to shepherd and guide and instruct].*

> —Ephesians 4:11 AMP

Certain people are set to be in the fivefold positions of apostles, prophets, evangelists, pastors, and teachers. Some will never fulfill their destiny, even though they're called to it. Some people in hell should have been in each fivefold position. They never came to the knowledge of Christ, and, in turn, never operated in their fivefold calling. That hurts the body because the church needs everyone to participate and function in their calling.

I want to encourage you to pray that the Spirit of God allows you to participate in these gifts. I pray that I will operate in all of them. I have operated in many of the gifts at different times. When God needs me to operate in a particular gift, then it will come forth.

I don't particularly claim to operate in any certain one continually, because I believe that the Holy Spirit can use people as He sees fit at the time. I never want to limit Him. We know that certain people have specific gifts, and those are notable. However, I don't believe that you should form your ministry off the gifts.

Now, going back to revelation of the now, and specifically words of knowledge, when I say *word*, it means just that. It is a word, and you can picture it like bullet points with a single word or phrase that God gives you. These words may be foreknowledge or knowledge that there's no way you could have known. Or it could be information that you are familiar with, but God is telling you to release it right now. It doesn't have to be new information, but to the person or to the congregation you're speaking to, it has meaning and speaking it will be profound.

The Lord may give you these words differently; however, for me, it typically happens after I've been reading or studying and then move onto the next topic. Once I have moved on, the Lord gives me a prophetic word.

WORDS OF KNOWLEDGE TEND THE HEART

Then He spoke many things to them in parables, saying: "Behold, a sower went out to sow. And as he sowed, some seed fell by the wayside; and the birds came and devoured them. Some fell on stony places, where they did not have much earth; and they immediately sprang up because they had no depth of earth. But when the sun was up they were scorched, and because they had no root they withered away. And some fell among thorns, and the thorns sprang up and choked them. But others fell on good ground and yielded a crop: some a hundredfold, some sixty, some thirty. He who has ears to hear, let him hear!"

—Matthew 13:3–9

This happens at every Spirit School. People may not realize it, but every Friday night service is a prophetic service. The Lord has instructed me to tend to the soil of people's hearts. It probably sounds like I am just speaking on random subjects, but God is actually giving me, word for word, what to say to help position people's hearts to receive from Him.

Four types of soil are mentioned in Matthew 13, and when I'm preparing for the Friday night service, the Lord will begin to speak to me. "Kevin, you're going to talk about this and this. Get Scriptures on this subject, this subject, and this subject. Tell this story. Then go this way with it."

So instead of calling people out, where I would only be able to get to a few people, the Lord gives me words of knowledge that I then weave through the service in order to help tend hearts by addressing subjects like forgiveness, trauma, and rejection. These are the rocks, thorns, and briars that Jesus is referring to in this parable.

WORDS THAT LEAD AND GUIDE

God gave me words of knowledge often, even from the time I first became a Christian. Right after I got saved, I began attending a Bible-believing, Spirit-filled church. I went to a weekly Bible study where I would get very accurate and profound words of knowledge for people. I didn't understand it, but as soon as I had been baptized in the Holy Spirit, it began happening.

One week, the leader got frustrated and pulled me aside to tell me that he was the leader, and since I was a brand-new Christian, God wouldn't be speaking to me. He would be speaking to him as the group leader.

This was an uncomfortable situation, and he seemed to be intimated, like I was usurping his position, especially since many young people were in the group. Of course, that wasn't my intention. I was a new believer, and the things of God were so real to me. He told me not to give any more words or pray for people, and that God would use him.

I agreed to that because I was a young Christian, and I believed he was just giving me instructions. As he was speaking to me about this, I began having an open vision. Everything disappeared, and I was outside on the sidewalk, looking down at the edging of grass between the sidewalk and the lawn. Down in the gap, I saw a brown leather wallet, and the Lord said to me, "Go get that wallet. It belongs to him."

I came out of the vision and immediately walked outside to the location that I was shown, which was down the street a bit. I looked down, and there it was, right where I had seen it. I picked it up and opened it, and sure enough, it was this pastor's wallet. Moments ago, the Lord had shown it to me in a vision, and here it was in my hand.

So I walked back in and handed it to him. It had been missing since the last Bible study. I told him that the Lord showed me where it was. After that, he never discouraged me from giving words, and he was then convinced that God was using me.

Through the revelation of the now, God can give you guidance. He can give you a word. These words may be for you and your life, but mostly, they will be for other people. When I get around people, the Lord begins to give me words for them. At times, He has told me to encourage someone in a particular direction. I won't tell them the word because I don't want people to become dependent on me for the direction of their life, but over the next year, I will work toward getting them in that direction. So at times, I know things ahead of time, but I don't say anything. Other times, I share the information with a leader who is responsible for the person I have the word for.

Another way that this gift manifests is when I am praying about something happening in my body. For example, I was praying in the spirit, and suddenly, I got a word in English that I was not familiar with, a scientific term. I looked it up and it was a supplement. I started taking it, and the issue I was having was healed. This has happened to Kathi and me several times.

Other times, when the Lord has given me a word in a certain situation, I will find a piece of information that I need. When I first became a Christian, I was looking for a certain running program. I wanted to increase my performance and my time in certain races. I was a long-distance runner, but I would run in track-and-field relay races as well.

So the Lord gave me guidance with a word, and I looked it up. The book that came up had different training profiles to increase your running time and performance. It had a whole year of training regimens, and by following the recommendations, I was able to set school records and get into state championships for track and field.

TENDING YOUR SPIRITUAL LIFE

Another important aspect that I mentioned in chapter one is that when I spend time studying Scripture and researching different subjects in the Bible, the Holy Spirit can use that later. He will give me subjects to study; I will read and meditate on hundreds of Scriptures that the Spirit will pull from and use later.

It's so important to tend to your spiritual life. At times, when I am lacking spiritually, I am not able to operate in the fullness of the gifts of the Spirit. All gifts are from the Spirit, and He gives you that ability. Still, I have noticed that if I'm not tending to my spiritual life, I get squeezed dry.

In order to operate in your giftings, you must be at an optimum level spiritually. That means that you're going to have to be watchful that satan is not attacking you so that you rise up in the flesh.

Over the years, I have seen satan preemptively attack people. Within hours or even minutes after he attacks you, you will come across someone that you need to minister to, and the Lord uses you. But I can see that satan knew that was going to happen, and he tried to get me off track.

> *There is therefore now no condemnation to those who are in Christ Jesus, who do not walk according to the flesh, but according to the Spirit.*

> —Romans 8:1

Romans 8 is a template for your life. We are to walk in the Spirit and not in the flesh. Galatians 5:16 says that walking in the Spirit prevents us from fulfilling the lust of the flesh and that the desires of the Spirit are contrary to the flesh and vice versa—they are at war with each other.

If you find yourself walking in the flesh, fulfilling the lust of the flesh, it will hinder your giftings, especially words of knowledge and words of wisdom. God wants to use you in ministry in an amazing way, and you must be watchful because the attacks of the enemy are preemptive at times. You must be aware of what is working against you, and if you find yourself in a scenario or situation where you are being tested, be careful. Familiar spirits are trying to knock you out and prevent you from working with God and fulfilling His will.

God wants to use this gift through you. He will give you words when you lay hands on people. You will either be led to speak forth what you are hearing, or the Spirit will lead you in the direction you are to pray.

Chapter 4

Supernatural Understanding: Word of Wisdom

Wisdom is the principal thing; therefore get wisdom. And in all your getting, get understanding. Exalt her, and she will promote you; she will bring you honor, when you embrace her. She will place on your head an ornament of grace; a crown of glory she will deliver to you.

—Proverbs 4:7–9

The word of wisdom, another gift of the Spirit, is for the days ahead and is connected to visitation. Solomon addresses wisdom extensively in Proverbs. This verse talks about getting wisdom and getting understanding. For me, this highlights the difference between a word of *knowledge* and a word of *wisdom*. A word of knowledge would be a fact or bullet point about a situation—it is informational. A word of wisdom, however, is the understanding of how to navigate a circumstance. It is counsel from the Lord when He gives you insight into what is going on. The Lord has often shown me a perspective from above—a bird's-eye view of what is happening. I see the whole situation in a flash.

WISDOM PREPARES US

One example of being given a word of wisdom is when the Lord warned me of what was to come prior to the COVID-19 pandemic. The Lord showed me that there would be shutdowns. He visited me and led me to form home fellowships and food pantries, and the Lord emphasized that He wanted me to create a homeschool curriculum. I felt the urgency of this word and knew I needed to act quickly.

Creating our homeschool curriculum has been a huge endeavor, but it is very important to the Lord because the enemy is targeting children by infiltrating the school systems with the spirit of the world. Since launching our homeschool curriculum, we have been able to produce a grade per year. Currently, we have six completed homeschool grades, as well as an online school of ministry where students can pursue their associate's, bachelor's, master's, and doctoral degrees. Our goal is to be able to bring children from kindergarten all the way to their doctorate.

Within a year of being visited by the Lord and acting on His warnings, we began to experience the effects of the pandemic: shutdowns, rioting, and food shortages. The Lord gave me many words of knowledge during that season, but He also gave me wisdom on how to respond and how to mobilize Warrior Notes in anticipation of these global events.

The Lord showed me that much of what I saw was conditional. We could pray against these coming troubles, and He showed me what He wanted for our nation. The church was not in its proper place and was allowing these events to happen through inaction. We must continue to pray against every terrible event that is still pending.

Much of what the Lord showed me during that season did come to pass, including cities burning, looting, election fraud, the manufacturing of diseases, and attacks on the police. This was not God's perfect will, but He warned me that this would happen if the church did not take authority and repent for the nation.

When the Lord showed me what was to come, He also led me to buy many different items. I purchased bulk amounts of toilet paper, disinfectants, canned foods, etc. This wasn't God's perfect will, but during that time, God still wanted His people to prosper and give us wisdom and counsel as to the steps to take.

ADHERING TO HIS WISDOM

During this pandemic season, at times, we weren't allowed to meet in convention centers, but I was able to broadcast every week from our studios, and we never lost any momentum.

All this is God's wisdom, and we must adhere to it. The Lord showed me that we must boost our immune systems and led me to hire healthcare professionals and begin teaching about general health to be wise and strengthen our physical bodies.

WARRIOR FELLOWSHIPS AND OUTREACHES

And they continued steadfastly in the apostles' doctrine and fellowship, in the breaking of bread, and in prayers. Then fear came upon every soul, and many wonders and signs were done through the apostles.

—Acts 2:42–43

The global pandemic and the spirit of the antichrist that is in opposition through corrupt people in government affected many local church bodies. Churches were not able to meet, which disrupted their finances and impacted their ability to help the local community. As a result, many churches are still paralyzed and ineffective.

After receiving God's warnings, I understood that He wanted to use Warrior Notes to help people by anticipating their needs. This led to the formation of our weekly Warrior Fellowships, which are hosted by Warrior Notes School of Ministry graduates. They consist of a weekly Bible study and outreach to the community. Many of the fellowships are becoming churches, and the leaders are becoming pastors. Through ministry expansion, we can meet the needs of the local community. We are seeing people saved and brought into the body of Christ.

Every generation has a movement where people come out of denominations that have grown cold and become ineffective and return to home fellowships. We see this cycle that helps bring the church back into the marketplace to share the gospel. We are in this cycle again, and Warrior Notes has become part of the catalyst for this. The Warrior Notes Fellowships were based on the wisdom that God gave me in this vision at night when He visited me and gave me an understanding of the state of the church and His plan for the days ahead.

WISDOM IS SUPERNATURAL

A word of wisdom from the Lord will be a practical solution for a particular situation. Different types of dynamics may relate to your job, church, family, or anything else in your life. The situation you are in may be controversial or possibly not working correctly. You may not know what to do, but God will bring the word of wisdom in a moment so that you understand all the dynamics. This is supernatural, and you will suddenly know what is going on and what you are supposed to do. We need wisdom and understanding of what to do in these situations, and we must be prayerful and allow the Lord to speak to us.

In a word of wisdom, He gave me the understanding that now is the time to write this book because people need greater revelation as we enter these next seasons of change in our country and the world.

> *That the God of our Lord Jesus Christ, the Father of glory, may give to you the spirit of wisdom and revelation in the knowledge of Him, the eyes of your understanding being enlightened; that you may know what is the hope of His calling, what are the riches of the glory of His inheritance in the saints, and what is the exceeding greatness of His power toward us who believe, according to the working of His mighty power which He worked in Christ when He raised Him from the dead and seated Him at His right hand in the heavenly places, far above all principality and power and might and dominion, and every name that is named, not only in this age but also in that which is to come. And He put all things under His feet, and gave Him to be head over all things to the church, which is His body, the fullness of Him who fits all in all.*

—Ephesians 1:17–23

Paul prayed this for the people at Ephesus. The city of Ephesus was one of the capitals of witchcraft, and the people were steeped in it. Paul prayed that they would be flooded with light, that the spirit of wisdom and revelation, in the knowledge of Jesus, would be given to them. I want to pray this for you as well, that you will operate in this gift, and it will help you and those around you with your life situations.

When you speak with your friends and family or run into someone in the marketplace, you'll talk to them, and God will give you insight. It may be a word of knowledge first, but then a word of wisdom will come, and you will begin explaining the spiritual environment to them. So I also pray the prayer from Ephesians 1:17–18 for myself and others.

I've seen the spiritual environments and stages in people's lives; I've seen what they're going through right now. The Lord will open this up to me; suddenly, I am mindful of what's going on with people. Of course, I don't know everything, and if I don't know something, I will wait to speak and move.

I remain silent for a time, but then suddenly, the Lord shows me and reveals that it is time for something to happen and gives me understanding. I believe that you are supposed to operate in this as well. God has this in mind for the days ahead: words of wisdom and supernatural revelation of the future.

Chapter 5

Creating Altars in Your Home

When Abram was ninety-nine years old, the Lord appeared to Abram and said to him, "I am Almighty God; walk before Me and be blameless. And I will make My covenant between Me and you, and will multiply you exceedingly." Then Abram fell on his face, and God talked with him, saying: "As for Me, behold, My covenant is with you, and you shall be a father of many nations. No longer shall your name be called Abram, but your name shall be Abraham; for I have made you a father of many nations."

—Genesis 17:1–5

When I was with Jesus in the heavenly realm, I saw that the family unit is the most important relationship, second only to our relationship with God. Our relationships with our family and the home where we live greatly affect us. Whether or not we like it, people and situations that we are involved with affect our relationship with God.

God changes you when He chooses to move on you, touch you, and reveal Himself to you. When this happens, you become born again, and you start to receive the things of God. God impacts your life, and then you begin to impact those around you.

When Abraham became a God-follower, that relationship influenced him so much that Abraham's whole family worshipped God. When God moves on people, the whole family is influenced, and the household is saved. That's God's will. His intention from the beginning was to have a family.

After the fall, we see that some of Adam's children served God, and some did not. We can follow different lineages—some bloodlines became evil and disappeared as they worked against God. Interbreeding happened with Cain and his line.

We can follow the sons of God, who were the sons of Adam. As we track their history, we witness the first murder. We begin to see stealing, killing, and destroying happening in Cain's line. We can identify that the seed of the serpent was at work. By the time we get to Genesis 6, interbreeding is going on. By chapter 7, we are with Noah as the earth is flooded and destroyed.

We can continue reading as Nimrod comes on the scene; Babylon is formed, and races of giants pop up again. By the time of King David, there are wars with the hybrid races, and Goliath is defeated. All throughout this journey, we watch as the patriarchs of faith build altars to the Lord.

When you make your home an altar, you set your home and yourself apart, creating a sacred space where God can meet with you. You must get back to a more intimate relationship with God, and then He will begin to work in your life.

For as I was passing through and considering the objects of your worship, I even found an altar with this inscription: TO THE UNKNOWN GOD.

Therefore, the One whom you worship without knowing, Him I proclaim to you: God, who made the world and everything in it, since He is Lord of heaven and earth, does not dwell in temples made with hands.

—Acts 17:23–24

When Paul came across this altar, he used it as a jumping point to preach the gospel and influence the people toward God. Throughout Acts, we see many pagan altars and temples where people worshiped false gods. Our culture has begun to return to pagan worship, and we must become a stronger influence.

The bottom line is that worshipping God begins in your home and with your family. You allow God to influence you and your family. Then your family begins to influence the community, and the community influences the city, and the cities influence the states, and eventually, the states can influence the country. The enemy is working overtime to try to influence and destroy the family unit. God wants to build up the family unit because it is the core of the nation.

THE GOD OF ABRAHAM, ISAAC, AND JACOB

Then Abram went up from Egypt, he and his wife and all that he had, and Lot with him, to the South. Abram was very rich in livestock, in silver, and in gold. And he went on his journey from the South as far as Bethel, to the place where his tent had been at the beginning, between Bethel and Ai, to the place of the altar which he had made there at first. And there Abram called on the name of the LORD.

—Genesis 13:1–4

Abraham built an altar and met with God, and later, Issac is in the same location. He, too, worshiped the Lord (Genesis 26:17–25). Finally, Jacob ends up in the same land by default, but he did not realize he was following in his father's and grandfather's steps. While Jacob was on his journey, the sun went down, and he had to stay the night in an unfamiliar place. He gathered rocks from all around, lay down, and went to sleep. While he was asleep, he had a dream and saw a ladder with the angels ascending and descending. Jacob suddenly realized that God was in that place.

Then Jacob awoke from his sleep and said, "Surely the LORD is in this place, and I did not know it." And he was afraid and said, "How awesome is this place! This is none other than the house of God, and this is the gate of heaven!"

—Genesis 28:16–17

Jacob should have known that God was in that place because there, his grandfather had opened the gate to Heaven through an altar. Isaac had honored that, but then Jacob didn't. We find ourselves in this same situation today. We have this mindset that we go to church in a church building with all this sophisticated equipment and media. People are processed through the church buildings. This is dictated by culture because not too long ago, we didn't have cell phones or quality audio-visual equipment.

Some groups of people, like the children of Israel, entered the desert as one large community. In the early church, they didn't have church buildings; the people met in their homes. Similarly, in the time of Jesus, the Jewish community rejected Him. The community would meet in synagogues and at the temple. Jesus was expelled, so He went into the fields. He never had His own building; He preached on hilltops and shores and then met in people's homes (Matthew 5:1; Luke 5:1).

Culture has changed so much, and now we function in a corporate setting, maintain a church building, abide by laws and rules about taxes, etc. In times of trouble and persecution, Christians migrate back to the home church setting. We recently experienced this during the pandemic shutdowns; churches were not permitted to meet. Church finances were affected by the closures. There has been some recovery in the past four years, but many churches never recovered and permanently closed.

> *Jesus said to her, "Woman, believe Me, the hour is coming when you will neither on this mountain, nor in Jerusalem, worship the Father. You worship what you do not know; we know what we worship, for salvation is of the Jews. But the hour is coming, and now is, when the true worshipers will worship the Father in spirit and truth; for the Father is seeking such to worship Him. God is Spirit, and those who worship Him must worship in spirit and truth."*

> —John 4:21–24

At Jacob's well, Jesus spoke to the Samaritan woman and told her that the time was coming when no one would worship God on this mountain or any mountain. Today, the Jewish people don't have a place of worship. Many Christian churches have closed, and this is part of the cycle that we are in. However, we must understand that the altar can be built anywhere.

Abraham found himself building an altar. Jesus built an altar wherever he was. He taught the people, and then he fed and prayed for them. Jesus traveled to many different places and homes as He ministered. We can follow this through the book of Acts, where there were instances of three thousand and five thousand people being saved (Acts 2:41; 4:4). This community of believers was being persecuted; they met in their homes, and the early church grew and expanded exponentially.

YOU ARE A LIVING SACRIFICE

Therefore I urge you, brothers and sisters, by the mercies of God, to present your bodies [dedicating all of yourselves, set apart] as a living sacrifice, holy and well-pleasing to God, which is your rational (logical, intelligent) act of worship.

—Romans 12:1 AMP

As Paul says here in Romans, we are to be living sacrifices, holy and acceptable, which is spiritual worship. As a believer, you are born again of the Spirit, and you have become a living sacrifice, an altar. Wherever you are, you can build an altar and allow God to show up.

Meditate on what Paul is saying here. Present your physical body as a living sacrifice as an act of spiritual worship. There is a transference from the physical to the spiritual. Now imagine what God can exchange in the reverse direction, from the spiritual to the physical.

Presenting yourself as a living sacrifice sets you apart and begins the interchange between spirit and body. The next thing that happens is that you are able to discern—discern when things are good or not good in their origin (1 John 4:1). This is one of the benefits of having an altar within. You turn yourself in and self-correct. The altar will get you into spiritual alignment. You don't need to get it all right before coming to the altar, but you should expect that God will make you right when you get up from the altar.

> *We have an altar from which those who serve the tabernacle have no right to eat.*

> —Hebrews 13:10

In the Old Testament, only the priest was permitted to engage in certain acts of worship. He alone could enter the holy of holies and was the only person who could partake of the table of the Lord. Within the tabernacle, the priests would pass through different stages. Common people were not allowed to enter, and even the priest was restricted in how he could walk through each stage of the worship process.

Under the new covenant, you don't want to be restricted to all the old because you've been given access under the new covenant. The veil has been torn, and now you can access the holy of holies. Not only are altars available, but you can go in and present yourself as a living sacrifice there.

You turn yourself into an altar, and then you are permitted to enter the inner chambers of the tabernacle. You may eat of the showbread. You may wash your hands in the bronze laver, and then you are permitted to enter the holy of holies. This needs to be preached more in today's churches so that we have this reality that we've come a long way through Jesus Christ. We ought to see more results from our warfare as we stand firm. We should see more supernatural events in our lives.

Chapter 6

Becoming an Outpost

Are they not all ministering spirits sent out to serve for the sake of those who are to inherit salvation?

—Hebrews 1:14 ESV

The Lord showed me that He wants to turn your territory, where you live, into an outpost for supernatural activity. God wants you and your territory to experience the angelic and all kinds of amazing events.

I want to caution you that once you hear this, it will become apparent that you're in a war, and ultimately, you are responsible for that knowledge. Warfare is occurring even if you are aware of it, but as you read on, you will desire to know and understand your role to a greater extent.

I get concerned when people take a casual approach to this serious matter. Prior to my heavenly visitation, I didn't know very much about these topics, and I was guessing at many of them. When the Lord pulled back the curtain and showed me what was going on behind the scenes, I was actually shocked, and I didn't want to come back.

This is because, as you begin to learn about warfare and territories, you must not be casual about it. Often, we are bombarded with religious spirits, and in many religious circles, people have grown cold and become dull regarding their knowledge of the spirit realm; as a result, satan has a heyday with many Christians.

PATHWAY TO THE ANGELIC

Angels are looking for locations where they can work. When this revelation came to me, I was living in my Phoenix home. I had created a beautiful garden in my backyard. There was an area to build a fire and a flagstone path that wound through the garden. I would spend hours walking on these paths, praying in a sort of prayer walk. Often, I would wake up at 3:00 or 4:00 a.m. and go out to my garden path to pray.

One night, after dark, I had just finished eating, and I was out there. Kathi was in the kitchen, cleaning up the dishes. I told her, "I need to go and pray. I'll be back in a little bit." I went out and started praying. I don't know exactly how long it took before this happened, but I turned and walked through this pathway in my backyard.

As I stepped on the path, suddenly, the whole backyard just lit up, even though it had been pitch black. I began feeling movement around me, and it was all good. As I kept walking, my eyes began to open, and I saw these forms that looked like angels. They were bright beings. Some were walking, and some were standing. There were about thirty in total. In my heart, I asked the Lord what was going on. As they walked near me, I felt incredible power, and I couldn't understand what was happening.

I began to ask them questions. I asked what they were doing. One of them answered, "Because you have prayed and done warfare here, your home has been chosen as an outpost in the northern part of the city. We have been assigned to a minister (they named the minister). He is here speaking at the convention center downtown."

The conference was supposed to start in a day or two, but I didn't know anything about it. Afterward, I looked it up, and sure enough, that minister was speaking in town that weekend. The angels explained that they were on assignment to assist in people's salvation.

I was in shock, but the angels instructed me to continue praying, and so I did. The power of God in my backyard was amazing and seemed out of this world.

This story is important to share because it was such a revelation that the angels would set up a command center because of a believer's prayers.

> *The weapons of our warfare are not physical [weapons of flesh and blood]. Our weapons are divinely powerful for the destruction of fortresses. We are destroying sophisticated arguments and every exalted and proud thing that sets itself up against the [true] knowledge of God, and we are taking every thought and purpose captive to the obedience of Christ.*

—2 Corinthians 10:4–5 AMP

This is an important Scripture. Not many Scriptures directly address spiritual warfare. There is a lot we do not know, and certain aspects of this appear to have been hidden from us. We don't have as much information about the demonic and the other realms as we'd like. So we should really focus on the Scriptures we do have.

Human beings can be used as puppets, but there is a puppet master, and manipulation and power are going on behind the scenes. People are influenced by the unseen realm, which affects their behaviors and personalities.

On the other side with Jesus, I saw the manipulation that's going on behind the scenes. (I did not share this in my first book.) These secret influences are diabolical, and a lot more is happening than you would imagine.

This is why the church has become so ineffective in this generation. Christians do not understand the spiritual realm. Satan does not want us to focus on what Jesus did when He was seated at the right hand of God. If the enemy can distract us, we will not walk in the authority and power the Lord has provided over serpents, scorpions, and every evil work.

So what is our true role down here? Well, we are supposed to establish an altar in our homes and then establish a territory that can become an outpost where angels want to come.

Remember, the angels told me they chose my house and backyard for their command center because I had spent time engaging in spiritual warfare. Over the years, I had prayed for hundreds, perhaps thousands, of hours, and so they considered the land to be holy ground.

They looked forward to coming to that backyard. All I was doing was praying and minding my own business, and suddenly, the spirit realm opened up to me, and I realized that my backyard had become an outpost for my territory. Prior to this, I prayed and did not have this type of encouragement. The reality is, we pray, and we don't always see what is going on around us.

FALSE ACCUSATIONS

Second Corinthians 10:4–5 says that we are warring but not against human beings—flesh and blood—that we see. Instead, we're warring against spirits that are working behind the scenes as puppet masters. These spirits give people false ideas about themselves and about the devil and demons. They also degrade and falsely accuse human beings and place people out of the loop of true information.

> *Once you were dead because of your disobedience and your many sins. You used to live in sin, just like the rest of the world, obeying the devil—the commander of the powers in the unseen world. He is the spirit at work in the hearts of those who refuse to obey God. All of us used to live that way, following the passionate desires and inclinations of our sinful nature. By our very nature we were subject to God's anger, just like everyone else.*
>
> —Ephesians 2:1–3 NLT

False accusations are thoughts, and thoughts will influence behavior and personality. People in the world have no resistance to this process, as Paul explains in Ephesians 2. The only way that we can overcome the influence is to be born again and begin to walk in the Spirit.

If we go back and further examine 2 Corinthians 10:4–5, we can see now that God has given us divine power to destroy strongholds, arguments, and anything that exalts itself above the knowledge of Christ. We bring every thought—even a single thought!—into captivity to the obedience of Christ.

When I was in Heaven, I saw that we must be careful when we are dealing with people in the world. You cannot fully trust people who are not Christians because they don't have any way of withstanding or engaging in spiritual warfare.

> *I fed you with milk, not solid food; for you were not yet able to receive it. Even now you are still not ready. You are still worldly [controlled by ordinary impulses, the sinful capacity]. For as long as there is jealousy and strife and discord among you, are you not unspiritual, and are you not walking like ordinary men [unchanged by faith]?*

—1 Corinthians 3:2–3 AMP

Here, Paul is talking about the path of maturity that believers take when they come out of the world. People who are of the world act just like the devil because they're children of the devil (John 8:44). Essentially, we were all children of satan until we got saved, and then we severed our ties with the spirit of the world, but we are still in a war.

At certain times in church history, the church seems to have become ineffective because we don't discern the spirit realm. We don't discern that God wants our territory to become an outpost for angelic activity and support for His will to be accomplished.

We are to engage in warfare, destroying arguments and anything raised above the knowledge of Christ. Take what's in the Bible and hold it up to a situation, conversation, or a person's character; if it doesn't add up to what's in the Word, it must be addressed.

If this isn't happening and if Christians don't mature, they become carnal and get washed out. These Christians begin to participate in the spirit of the world. Paul addressed this and explained that people who operate in that cannot inherit the kingdom of God.

Do you not know that the unrighteous will not inherit the kingdom of God? Do not be deceived. Neither fornicators, nor idolaters, nor adulterers, nor homosexuals, nor sodomites, nor thieves, nor covetous, nor drunkards, nor revilers, nor extortioners will inherit the kingdom of God.

—1 Corinthians 6:9–10

All these activities that Paul lists are things you would do in the world before you were a Christian. However, Paul was addressing the people in the church. When I was growing up, I was taught that this Scripture was referring to the world. I see that this is a type of deception, which is why we bring everything into captivity and to the obedience of Christ.

THE CHURCH DEFENDS ITS TERRITORY

Finally, my brethren, be strong in the Lord and in the power of His might. Put on the whole armor of God, that you may be able to stand against the wiles of the devil. For we do not wrestle against flesh and blood, but against principalities, against powers, against the rulers of the darkness of this age, against spiritual hosts of wickedness in the heavenly places. Therefore take up the whole armor of God, that you may be able to withstand in the evil day, and having done all, to stand.

—Ephesians 6:10–13

God wants Christians to take territory and turn it into an outpost. It begins with you and your family in your home. Then, groups of believers build each other up. To do this, we need strong churches with mature people. We need the five-fold ministry to build up the body into maturity so we are full of faith and become a spiritual outpost. If churches become ineffective, they will never become outposts. Smaller groups and individuals will need to step in the churches' place and become effective and hot. Intercessors will need to carry the load for that territory.

We are encouraged to be strong in the Lord and in the strength of His might. We must put on the full armor of God so that we can stand against the schemes of the enemy. The word *stand* is repeated several times, and it means we are defending our stance, our position. With the exception of the sword of the Spirit, the rest of the armor is all defensive.

You have territories, and you must defend them. You are to become an outpost so that you are able to stand against the battle strategies of the devil. Defend what has been assigned to you; establish your authority and allow the angelic to come in and help you minister to those who will inherit salvation.

Chapter 7

Visitations of Angels

Do not neglect to extend hospitality to strangers [especially among the family of believers—being friendly, cordial, and gracious, sharing the comforts of your home and doing your part generously], for by this some have entertained angels without knowing it.

—Hebrews 13:2 AMP

God has revealed many things to me regarding angels. Unfortunately, this topic has become sensationalized. People really want to hear about angels because they are exciting, but many of the stories that have been told are fabrications and unbiblical. My desire is to remain balanced.

I would rather study the Word, pray, prophesy, and just be a teacher and an evangelist and then allow the angels to come as they are sent. Whether or not I have an angelic visitation, whether or not I hear God's voice, I still go about my day and follow the last instruction I received from the Lord.

It's similar to when I am flying. At times, I may lose communication with the controller due to the weather or other factors. I don't worry when this happens because I already have my instructions. I have my flight plan, and I understand the instruments and the effects of weather on the airplane. I am trained and have what I need, so I am confident that if I lose radio communication, I know I can follow my flight plan and rely on my instruments.

So whether or not you have a supernatural experience doesn't change your assignment and what you already know. You still go to work and carry on as normal. It is easy to get into error when you want something to happen. I must be very careful in my life and in teaching to make sure that what I say doesn't contribute to creating a desire within you for these experiences. I want you to desire the Lord Himself and base your faith on the Word and on the Spirit of God.

Then, along that path, you may have angelic visitations. But to tell you the truth, what I saw on the other side is that every Christian has angels around them and has encountered angels many times. The angels are hidden because they don't want to be known. They want God to get the glory, and they don't draw attention to themselves. They consider it a job well done when they remain anonymous.

You are having angelic visitations and receiving their help all the time. However, you should know that you can take practical steps to assist angels in their work.

Hebrews 13:2 mentions angels, but it also refers to ministers and those people you entertain who are on an assignment. At times, the angels have tested me to see how I would respond before disappearing. Often, it occurs when I offer food or other types of help. The angels were just observing me to see, and it was a test.

Some people around you have needs, and you should be aware that the Holy Spirit may be guiding you. It's important not to override that prompt because at times, that's when I've had these angelic visitors who were observing me, and they were actually monitoring the situation.

Angels do not want attention drawn to them, and they do not want to be worshiped. They are here to help us, and they help immensely. They are behind the scenes and don't want any credit.

> *God sends angels with special orders to protect you wherever you go, defending you from all harm. If you walk into a trap, they'll be there for you and keep you from stumbling.*
>
> —Psalm 91:11–12 TPT

Psalm 91 shows us that angels are on assignment. Some are over territories, and they watch and monitor the area. Others are sent to minister and serve you for the sake of those who are to inherit salvation.

If you are a Christian and believe in your heart and confess with your mouth that Jesus is Lord, then you are saved, and you will inherit salvation (Romans 10:9–10). However, the Scripture says that we have the Holy Spirit as a deposit, which guarantees our full payment in the future. We are engaged, but the Lord will come back, and we will have a wedding. The indication is that we have not received full payment yet.

> *And because of him, when you who are not Jews heard the revelation of truth, you believed in the wonderful news of salvation. Now we have been stamped with the seal of the promised Holy Spirit. He is given to us like an engagement ring, as the first installment of what's coming! He is our hope-promise of a future inheritance which seals us until we*

have all of redemption's promises and experience complete freedom—all for the supreme glory and honor of God!

—Ephesians 1:13–14 TPT

Of course, we haven't overcome everything, and we still experience the effects of the curse on the earth. Certain laws are in motion, our lifespan is limited, and we do not live forever. We still must work by the sweat of our brows, and we must maintain our physical health. It's not all going to come naturally. We must manage certain areas of our lives and govern our finances. Additionally, there is an element of maintaining our freedom through deliverance. We must stay on top of the demonic and keep enforcing our authority in this area. It all requires focused attention and work.

The angels on assignment are for the unsaved but also for us who are saved; they are here to help us while we are on earth.

Angels won't always appear to you and give you a message. Sometimes, they just show up and act, and you think, *I have no idea what just happened, but God just did a miracle.*

At times, the angels come into a corporate gathering and change everything. I have experienced this many times during the Warrior Notes Spirit Schools. They will show up and change the entire direction of the service, and the atmosphere will shift in the room.

An angel will sometimes stand beside someone, and I will know to go to the person and release a word over them. In one instance, we were in Dalton, Georgia, in a conference of thirteen hundred people. As I walked to one of the back sections, I saw an angel next to a man. I went to him and said, "You just told the Lord that if this minister is real, have him walk over to me and tell me, and I will give my life to you." This man began shaking; he got saved and delivered.

A similar situation happened in Australia. There was limited seating, and a family was standing against the wall, listening to the service. I saw an angel standing beside the family, and he was pointing at them. Then the Holy Spirit gave me a word of knowledge for them. I walked to them and shared what I had seen, which was that I saw them sitting at their kitchen table that morning, where they spontaneously decided to come to the conference. They cried out to the Lord and asked Him to speak through me to confirm their ministry and calling. They had been on the other side of Australia during breakfast and got on a plane to be there in the evening. It was a complete miracle. That has happened many times where it involved angels.

ANGELS ADMINISTER HEALING

I was dealing with terrible sinus issues. This went on for a few years, and occasionally, I would be too sick to fly for work. One day, I had to call out because the pressure in my sinuses was so bad that I would not have been able to fly because it could damage my eardrums.

Late in the evening, Kathi and I were in bed reading the Word. I looked up, and suddenly, I could see into the other realm. There was an angel, not very large, like a man but otherworldly. He walked in and came over to me. Without saying a word, he placed two fingers on my hand, and I felt the power from the angel go right through my body like an electric current. Immediately, I was completely well. The angel then turned around. When he reached my bedroom door, he turned to me and said, "That is how easy it is to be healed." Then he walked out.

Bless the LORD, ye his angels, that excel in strength, that do his commandments, hearkening unto the voice of his word.

—Psalm 103:20 KJV

At the time, I did not believe in or expect angelic encounters because there aren't many stories like that in the Bible. However, there are indications of angels working in the background, like the angel who stirred the water at Bethesda (John 5:2–4).

Again, angels do not want any attention, and they don't want you to focus your ministry on them. They would view it as a failure if they were getting that type of attention.

They are on assignment, and we do not command the angels. The word of the Lord sends them. The angels hearken unto His voice. They don't hearken unto your voice. When you pray Scripture or speak prophetically by the Spirit, you are speaking out God's will, and the angels will respond to that. They will listen to what you are saying when it aligns with their assignment.

The Lord sends angels with specific tasks. They are agents of the Lord who hide as strangers. They can operate in the spirit realm at lightning speed and without restriction. We, too, are God's ministers. We walk in the Spirit and have authority as children, but we see dimly and are subject to many of the boundaries of this world. Angels have the capacity to operate on higher spiritual planes than we do. Do not be misled: We work alongside the angels as we respond to God's voice and fulfill His will.

Chapter 8

Revelation of Deception

But even if we, or an angel from heaven, should preach to
you a gospel contrary to that which we [originally] preached
to you, let him be condemned to destruction!

—Galatians 1:8 AMP

A s I mentioned in the previous chapter, many people claim that they have had angelic encounters, but the encounters do not align with Scripture. These are deceptions. Paul says that any person or angel who comes with a different gospel is cursed. Paul spoke very emphatically against deceptive practices and deceptive theology.

I have been walking with the Lord for forty-four years, and over the years, I've learned about deception. There are many misconceptions, and I feel that this is one of the most important topics that I can share with you.

When I was with the Lord in Heaven, I saw that when the Holy Spirit speaks to us and nudges us regarding deception, many times, we override that inner knowing. We do this for several reasons. One is that the person who the deception is coming through is deemed credible.

They have more experience or authority. Maybe they are a highly trained and well-respected professional. But as you watch them, you sense that something isn't right. I have learned the hard way that it is vital that you step in.

Ask yourself why you don't trust the person. Then pray about a way of addressing that with the person, even if they are in authority or if you trust them and they have credibility.

I was once flying at night with a student pilot, and I let them fly the aircraft as I taught them. We were on approach into Tucson, a busy international airport with lots of activity. Military aircraft are stationed there, including an F-16 squadron. There are multiple runways parallel to one another. When there are three runways, there is a right, center, and left runway that are spaced out. However, you can have multiple airplanes coming in and even landing simultaneously next to each other.

You must be very careful in situations like these, and as a pilot, you need to remember a lot of details. For instance, if you have a large airliner in front of you, you cannot get too close because of the wake, and the vortices created in that path can affect a smaller plane like the one we were in. However, I briefed the student on this and allowed him to go ahead with the landing.

I watched the gauges and him as he began the approach. Suddenly, he got a bit lower than we had discussed during the instruction and got caught in the wake and the vortices from the wings of the large airliner ahead of us. We were in a bad situation, and this caused the plane to roll.

I was able to step in and get control of the airplane. If I hadn't, we would have been dead. Yes, this person was a student, but he had flown for a while. It's just one of those things where you have to be aware that a point may come when you have to take over and call out that something is wrong. In this case, I let it go past the point I should have.

I learned a huge lesson, and I learned it many times after that, both in aviation and also in other jobs. The lesson is that you must have a way out of a situation, taking over and calling out the mistake. We all make mistakes and miss things, and we need each other to stay accountable.

I've learned that deception occurs when you recognize that something is wrong, but because you think positively about the person and their status, etc., you allow it to go on longer than you should. I've done this with certain people, and it's gotten me into problematic situations that I could have prevented.

THE HOLY SPIRIT WANTS YOU TO BE SHARP

Do not be deceived, God is not mocked; for whatever a man sows, that he will also reap. For he who sows to his flesh will of the flesh reap corruption, but he who sows to the Spirit will of the Spirit reap everlasting life.

—Galatians 6:7–8

I want you to meditate on this verse and take it to heart. Paul is speaking to Christians, and this is the root of what I have been sharing. Don't be deceived: When a person is sowing to his flesh, it will result in fruit.

If God is in something, you will have the fruit of that, the fruit of the Spirit. But if the work of the flesh is involved—lying, cheating, stealing, etc.—if your property is being chronically broken, you must begin asking questions.

You must take care of it to avoid being deceived. God is a good God. Jesus went around doing good and healing everyone who was oppressed (Acts 10:38). Paul had a revelation of God's goodness and understood that it led people to repentance (Romans 2:4). The revelation of good causes people to turn, not the revelation of evil or hell.

> *Even so, every good tree bears good fruit, but a bad tree bears bad fruit. A good tree cannot bear bad fruit, nor can a bad tree bear good fruit. Every tree that does not bear good fruit is cut down and thrown into the fire. Therefore by their fruits you will know them.*
>
> —Matthew 7:17–20

Jesus told us that we can tell the type of tree by its fruit. So we can know ahead of time and don't have to be deceived. If we don't call out problems, we, along with many others, can be drawn in and hurt.

A lot of people have sown to the flesh, and then they reap destruction. We may wonder how it happened because they were so gifted or anointed, and they've been in ministry for forty years. We need to realize that it was happening the whole time. It didn't happen overnight. God is not mocked. You reap what you sow, and you cannot blame God when you reap a bad crop.

People are sometimes critical of Christians who believe in the full gospel, the gifts of the Spirit, and the charismatic movement. Some people don't believe in these practices. These people, cessationists, consider themselves to be born-again believers, but they do not believe in the ongoing works of the Holy Spirit. They believe that the gifts of the Spirit ended in the early church with the death of the apostles.

This is not true, and the Bible does not teach that. When I listen to some of these people, I have to agree with some of their criticisms because many charismatic preachers are teaching false doctrine.

We do have supernatural experiences and angelic visitations, but certain teachings on these subjects aren't true. It's the same way with the gifts of the Spirit. You cannot allow yourself to be deceived in the days ahead. The Holy Spirit wants us to display fruit. If someone's life does not display that fruit, it means they've been sowing to the flesh. Unfortunately, I have seen this happen repeatedly, and it is very disappointing. Some people have been deceived, but they've also deceived others because they were sowing to the flesh and getting a harvest. All the while, people around them ignored the warnings. This has been so hurtful to the body, and my goal in sharing this is to protect individuals and the body.

Whoever walks in integrity walks securely, but he who makes his ways crooked will be found out.

—Proverbs 10:9 ESV

If you walk in integrity, you'll be secure, and if your ways are crooked, you will be found out. What's happening here is that God, in His grace, allows this behavior for a certain amount of time, but then it all comes to light, and you will harvest what you have sown.

This is a hard message, but if we don't address the issue of deception, you will find out the hard way. The revelation the Holy Spirit gives us regarding deception is clear if you allow it to be. Do not permit yourself to push these issues aside and get yourself into trouble. When you see something wrong, when you see the fruit of the flesh, address it and don't allow it to continue to produce fruit.

At times, I have brought correction to individuals. I have had to tell people that they were not following biblical standards and could no longer be part of the ministry. Sometimes when the correction comes, there is repentance, and other times, there is not. Depending on the person's response, I will make the tough decision because I cannot allow those behaviors to propagate. Any deception that goes unchecked will give others the impression that those behaviors are acceptable when they are not.

As a leader, I must have high standards with a no-tolerance policy. Even the corporate environment has certain expectations and standards, usually outlined in handbooks that employees must agree to follow. However, I have encountered situations in churches and with ministries that would not have been tolerated for twenty-four hours at the corporate level. Yet in the church, this deception happens, and people believe that it's okay.

As a Christian, you stand out by your fruit. When I was an employee at Southwest Airlines, I wouldn't steal or lie. Even though this was in the handbook and one of the expectations of the job, it was very rare for individuals to have strong ethics like that. Southwest would fire staff for stealing, lying, or profanity, but I have seen all this going on in ministries, and it goes unaddressed. As Christians, we should stand out because we walk according to the fruit of the Spirit.

> *Do not be conformed to this world, but be transformed by the renewal of your mind, that by testing you may discern what is the will of God, what is good and acceptable and perfect.*
>
> —Romans 12:2 ESV

What is God's good and acceptable and perfect will? Jesus taught me that we must separate ourselves from the world. As we do this, we begin to have that revelation of deception because we're going to be separate from it.

First, you are separated, and then you are transformed. *Trans* refers to movement, such as *transportation*, and *formed* is a molding—we're changing form. This happens by renewing your mind by the Word of God. When you are transformed by renewing your mind, then you can test and discern what the will of God is.

In the days ahead, you must be willing to call out fruit that is not right. If something feels off and you get a warning in your spirit, you need to investigate it and align it with the fruit of the Spirit because God is not mocked.

Chapter 9

Supernatural Confirmation

For as many as are led by the Spirit of God, these are sons of God.

—Romans 8:14

At Warrior Notes, we focus on the individual relationship with God and then gathering to build one another up and have confirmation in the corporate anointing. This is why we have Spirit Schools and why we are moving forward with Warrior Ranches. We want to create environments for mentorship and fellowship.

The Lord showed me that He wants us to personally build ourselves up in the Holy Spirit and with the Word of God and that He wants to lead and guide us. As it says, each person is led by the Spirit. Those who are led by the Spirit are the sons of God—that's all of us. It's not just those in the fivefold ministry.

Over the years, there has been such an emphasis on the fivefold and the different tiers of authority. It has become a sort of cartel where those in authority are promoting each other's mutual interests and exploiting their influence.

*For, I think, God has exhibited us apostles at the end of the
line, like men sentenced to death [and paraded as prisoners
in a procession], because we have become a spectacle to the
world [a show in the world's amphitheater], both to angels
and to men.*

—1 Corinthians 4:9 AMP

It's funny, Paul claimed to be an apostle, and he described an apostle
as being at the end of the procession. He called them the "offscouring
of all things," and the lowest servant to all (1 Corinthians 4:13).

The apostle essentially fathered and mentored people and was not
a big authority figure. He didn't have authority over all the churches.
He only had authority over those who had placed themselves under
him. Churches were birthed from his preaching, and the emphasis on
authority was different than it is today.

The Word tells us that Jesus structured the church and the body
of Christ in such a way that the fivefold is responsible to minister to
the body (Ephesians 4:12). This ministry to the body brings the body
into maturity in the unity of the faith. This is the assignment of the
fivefold: to serve the body. The individuals are set in the church by
God to minister to His body so that the body is in place to go out and
minister to the world. The body is called to be the ministers, and the
fivefold are the servants who mentor, shape, and mature the larger
group.

I joke that the fivefold is supposed to be carrying your luggage.
They're supposed to be serving you. As the body matures, then we all
go out into the marketplace. We don't go witness—we are witnesses!
We are a demonstration of Jesus Christ in the marketplace through a
relationship with God. We are the salt that goes out.

These signs will accompany those who have believed: in My name they will cast out demons, they will speak in new tongues; they will pick up serpents, and if they drink anything deadly, it will not hurt them; they will lay hands on the sick, and they will get well.

—Mark 16:17–18 AMP

In this chapter, I want to focus on how God speaks to you individually through supernatural confirmation. These signs shall follow those who believe. It doesn't say these signs shall follow the fivefold ministers, yet look at the emphasis there is on the fivefold and whether or not they have miracles in their ministry. Then we put them up on a pedestal. But the miracles, the signs, will follow those who believe, which is everyone.

If I believe, then I don't have to be a fivefold minister to have miracles. Stephen wasn't a fivefold minister, and he had notable miracles. He waited tables and had uncommon miracles in his ministry. His words were so anointed that demons manifested when he spoke, and the Pharisees had him killed.

These signs will follow believers: They will raise the dead, cast out devils, and heal the sick. They will proclaim liberty and freedom (jubilee). Think about how awesome it could be for these signs and wonders to manifest for each of us.

However, Christians tend to point out certain individuals and follow them. It's okay to follow someone who is following the Lord, but the confirmation that you want to come through a minister should be from what God is already saying to you. Confirmation comes along afterwards. The whole body of Christ is supposed to be having this amazing personal relationship with God.

But when the truth-giving Spirit comes, he will unveil the reality of every truth within you. He won't speak on his own, but only what he hears from the Father, and he will reveal prophetically to you what is to come.

—John 16:13 TPT

Jesus said the Holy Spirit would come and be your counselor and helper. He's the Spirit of truth, which is another word for reality. He will lead you into all reality. Jesus goes on to say the Holy Spirit will remind you of things Jesus has said and reveal the future to you.

For you did not receive the spirit of bondage again to fear, but you received the Spirit of adoption by whom we cry out, "Abba, Father."

—Romans 8:15

We have the Spirit of adoption; the Holy Spirit gives us confirmation that we are adopted and the revelation of being children of God. Then, the Holy Spirit gives us hope. Remember, we spoke about receiving Him as a deposit that assures the full payment (Ephesians 1:14).

When we pray, we are talking to God. We don't know what to pray, but the Holy Spirit comes in, picks us up, and super-intercedes so that we pray out the perfect will of God. What could be better than that? We have the perfect will of God being prayed out because at times, we don't know what we should pray.

The Spirit, with non-articulate speech but rather with groanings, prays out the perfect will of God through us. So you find yourself speaking out the truth in the Spirit. You are praying out specific things, even though you don't know what you're saying. You are praying out mysteries. At some point, you are going to get what you're praying for. The confirmation will come through the gifts of the Spirit in someone else.

Words of knowledge and words of wisdom do not need to come through a prophet or another fivefold minister. Anyone in the body can operate in the gifts of the Spirit. First, you have a leading, and information has been given to you by the Spirit. Then you have confirmation through someone else—the process is supernatural. Whenever this happens, your faith and agreement increase.

In forty-four years, I would say I have experienced these confirmations innumerable times. I know that's a lot, but I've had so many confirmations when the Lord has just put something in my heart. It happens every day, several times per day, and then the confirmation comes.

In the Old Testament, people would ask for signs because they did not have the Holy Spirit inside them. God would give signs, such as supernatural occurrences in the climate and with the elements. In the New Testament, He is within us, and our confirmation comes through the Spirit.

In Phoenix, it doesn't rain very often. I don't go around praying, "Lord, there's no rain in the forecast. If you want me to do this, then make it rain today." God wants me to do what He has placed in my heart to do, but you can't depend on outside confirmations.

God doesn't use the natural elements. If you want to marry someone, then don't ask God to send an earthquake to confirm your decision. In the Old Testament, the Holy Spirit wasn't inside people like He is today. The Holy Spirit was upon the prophet, priest, and king. We can't look for outward signs to confirm something, and we can't depend upon prophets, apostles, or anyone else to give us a word that we haven't heard for ourselves.

If someone tells you brand new information, I wouldn't listen to it, and I don't. I've learned. I pray these matters out. At times, people have made statements that were way beyond my threshold of faith. I prayed about it, and the Lord showed me that it was true. In certain circumstances, this may happen to you as well. However, I would say that 99 percent of the time, a word given by someone else should be a confirmation.

FORMING YOUR MINDSET

He is the divine portrait, the true likeness of the invisible God, and the firstborn heir of all creation. For in him was created the universe of things, both in the heavenly realm and on the earth, all that is seen and all that is unseen. Every seat of power, realm of government, principality, and authority—it all exists through him and for his purpose! He existed before anything was made, and now everything finds completion in him.

He is the Head of his body, which is the church. And since he is the beginning and the firstborn heir in resurrection, he is the most exalted One, holding first place in everything. For God is satisfied to have all his fullness dwelling in Christ. And by the blood of his cross, everything in heaven and earth is brought back to himself—back to its original intent, restored to innocence again!

Even though you were once distant from him, living in the shadows of your evil thoughts and actions, he reconnected you back to himself. He released his supernatural peace to you through the sacrifice of his own body as the sin-payment on your behalf so that you would dwell in his presence. And now there is nothing between you and Father God, for he sees you as holy, flawless, and restored.

—Colossians 1:15–22 TPT

This is the foundation. I encourage you to print out these Scriptures and look at them, read them, and meditate on them. Every believer on earth needs to establish this proper order. I saw that God's plan was to bring humanity back to His original intent through Jesus Christ. This framework is the way things are supposed to be, that we are established through Jesus Christ. He is the One who made everything and then brought it back into order.

We don't see that original intent in the world, but we do see that in ourselves and in the church, or at least we are supposed to. The goal is that we all work together so that we are restored and Jesus is the head. When we are reconnected with Him, He then releases supernatural peace, which is shalom.

As a result of that sin payment through the blood, there is nothing between you and God. When we allow this process to occur, our relationship with each other will improve because we won't hinder each other or God. That's the proper order.

You will notice that Warrior Notes is a ministry that focuses on the body with corporate prayer. I do not lay hands on people too often. In the eight years since Kathi and I founded the ministry, we have felt strongly that we need to teach the body how to receive from God on their own and build one another up. This allows the confirmation of God's voice to come through one another.

The people in the body—not only the fivefold—should be the ministers who operate in signs and wonders. They are set in the church by God to serve the body; however, an overemphasis on the fivefold's importance has crept in. In Heaven, Jesus showed me that this has led the church into error. I thought, *It's going to be hard to change this mentality because we have become dependent on our leaders to hear from God for us and to give us guidance.*

Jesus Christ hung on the cross for all of us. We are all supposed to be kings and priests and are called as leaders in the body.

> *I can even celebrate the sorrows I have experienced on your behalf; for as I join with you in your difficulties, it helps you to discover what lacks in your understanding of the sufferings Jesus Christ experienced for his body, the church. This is the very reason I've been made a minister by the authority of God and a servant to his body, so that in his detailed plan I would fully equip you with the Word of God.*
>
> —Colossians 1:24–25 TPT

Another topic that's not being taught about is suffering. As Christians, we will suffer because Jesus suffered. Paul experienced this in his body, though. His assignment as an apostle is to fully equip the body.

> *There is a divine mystery—a secret surprise that has been concealed from the world for generations, but now it's being revealed, unfolded and manifested for every holy believer to experience. Living within you is the Christ who floods*

you with the expectation of glory! This mystery of Christ, embedded within us, becomes a heavenly treasure chest of hope filled with the riches of glory for his people, and God wants everyone to know it!

Christ is our message! We preach to awaken hearts and bring every person into the full understanding of truth. It has become my inspiration and passion in ministry to labor with a tireless intensity, with his power flowing through me, to present to every believer the revelation of being his perfect one in Jesus Christ.

—Colossians 1:26–29 TPT

Christ is our message! This is profound because this is what we're supposed to hear when we go to church; we're supposed to be hearing this mystery that has been revealed. This is the plan and the purpose that's been hidden in times past: The manifold wisdom of God would be revealed through the church.

Paul also talks about this in Ephesians 3:10. "To the intent that now the manifold wisdom of God might be made known by the church to the principalities and powers in the heavenly places." He is talking about God's manifold wisdom being shown to evil spirits in the heavenly realm through the body of Christ. This is true spiritual warfare and supernatural confirmation. When you walk in the Spirit, you will be continually confirming God's Word.

We are sons and daughters of destiny. We are destined for glory, but we also have that glory within us. That glory corrects and returns us to God's original intent. The glory of the Father that is coming upon the church in these last days will position us into the proper place.

Chapter 10

The Ultimate Enemy: Rejection

And they heard the sound of the LORD God walking in the garden in the cool of the day, and Adam and his wife hid themselves from the presence of the LORD God among the trees of the garden.

—Genesis 3:8

In the garden of Eden, Adam and Eve had everything. Everything was available to them; they had eternal life. They didn't die physically or spiritually. In my opinion, they didn't have to work or ask for things. Whatever they needed was just there; they could will it to happen. Their communication went beyond what we experience today. God would come down and talk with them. They just walked with Him.

When I was in the throne room in Heaven, I wasn't even allowed to look at the face of my Father. I could see His body up to a certain point, but I wasn't allowed to look at His face. The glory was in the throne room; the holiness, the righteousness, and the fear of the Lord were present. I was with Jesus, and I could look at Him but not at the face of the Father.

I think about the power of God demonstrated in the Old Testament. I think about some of the New Testament events that happened in the church when people died and were judged. I think that we forget that at one time, Adam and Eve could just walk with God and look at Him face-to-face. It was part of their daily life.

What they went through when they were sent out of the garden would have been unimaginable. They no longer had the same access to God, and they began to die. They began to have disagreements and had the ability to misunderstand. Their thought life was now different, and they could think and imagine things that they couldn't have before. They had to work, and they began to experience pain.

Everything that they experienced would have felt like rejection from God. They would have been thinking about this and overthinking it. They would have been trying to compensate. When I was with Him in Heaven, it was just so hard to come back to this earth, knowing the demonic that was here, instigating a lot of these problems. But I need you to understand this very important subject that the ultimate enemy is rejection.

Many disappointments and problems arise in life, and we sometimes go our whole lives without knowing why they occurred. However, God knows and understands everything. The hardest part for me over the years has been seeing what God wants for people and then knowing that it may not happen. This is so hard because people aren't living at the higher level that God wants. This lower level affects their health, relationships, provision, and everything in their life.

The ultimate enemy is rejection. Adam and Eve suffered greatly after the fall. The Old Testament also includes so many disconnects and horrible events, and sin is rampant. God had to bring the law through Moses just to keep people in order and in line because there was no other way to curb sin. Unless the law came, they wouldn't have even known what right and wrong was because they were so lost. That's how lost we are apart from Him.

> *"Teacher, which is the great commandment in the law?"*
> *Jesus said to him, "'You shall love the LORD your God with*
> *all your heart, with all your soul, and with all your mind.'*
> *This is the first and great commandment. And the second*
> *is like it: 'You shall love your neighbor as yourself.' On these*
> *two commandments hang all the Law and the Prophets."*
>
> —Matthew 22:36–40

We have laws, the military, police officers, judges, courts, etc., because people cannot be trusted to govern themselves. Remember, Jesus said that if you love your neighbor as yourself and you love God with all your heart, you fulfill all the commandments. We can fulfill all the commandments because they're all tied to loving God and loving our neighbor as ourselves. We look out for our neighbor. We also love God, so our loyalty is to Him, and we won't do anything that violates the greatest commandment.

Moses came to curb sin in the law. In Romans 8:3–4, Paul said, "For what the law could not do in that it was weak through the flesh, God did by sending His own Son in the likeness of sinful flesh, on account of sin." Jesus Christ became a sacrificial lamb for us and took upon Himself our punishment. We couldn't fulfill the law because we were lost.

The righteous requirement of the law was made through Jesus Christ, and now, we must live a certain way. We demonstrate positive behavior changes because of the Holy Spirit within us and begin to display the fruit of the Spirit. We have a personality change. The born-again experience is when our position and status are changed, and we become righteous. Then daily, we apply what we know. It's a walk of love and walking in the Spirit. We begin to see manifestations of God's love through miracles, provision, our own health, and healing others.

SPIRIT OF ACCEPTANCE

For you did not receive the spirit of bondage again to fear, but you received the Spirit of adoption by whom we cry out, "Abba, Father."

—Romans 8:15

The Spirit of God inside us always wants to confirm that we are children of God, we are loved, and we are accepted. He gives us a spirit of acceptance and adoption, and we become His children. We have been adopted and taken back; we've been accepted in and written back into God's will through Jesus Christ.

In this world, we're going to have troubles; we will possibly lose friends and family as many people choose not to follow God. It's very disappointing, especially after walking with God for a long time. I've seen people completely change, and it is heartbreaking. But you have an inheritance and adoption papers. You actually receive the same inheritance that Jesus received. However, believers need to process that you will naturally feel rejected as a result of the fall.

Being born again doesn't fix your soul—mind, will, and emotions. It only fixes your spirit. We must mature in Christ and grow up in Him (Colossians 1:28). Once your spirit gets saved, your soul needs transformation by the Word of God. Likewise, your body is not saved and still dies an earthly death at a certain age. It's a body of sin and it's corrupt. It's fallen. We no longer live forever like we did before the fall.

Now, your spirit lives forever, and you are born again. But your soul needs to be transformed, and your body needs to be corrected or disciplined. In 1 Corinthians 9:27, Paul said, "But I discipline my body and bring it into subjection, lest, when I have preached to others, I myself should become disqualified." In other words, by not disciplining himself, his body could be disqualified, which in the Greek means "to throw away or be put on the junk heap."[1] Can you imagine Paul getting knocked out of the race? Paul said he beat his body into submission so that wouldn't happen.

Let's recap. Your spirit is saved, but your soul needs to be transformed, and your body needs to be corrected or disciplined. You are made up of those three parts, and you also have the Spirit of God inside you, leading and guiding you and confirming that you are adopted as a child of God. When you go through these processes, it protects you and keeps you from entering cycles of rejection.

Our enemy is satan, and he was defeated through the salvation that Jesus bought. Jesus defeated the enemy on the cross, and the enemy has come to nothing. Jesus made a show of him openly, triumphing over him (Colossians 2:15). Now, satan is the one that's rejected, and all the demonic spirits, all those rogue, rebellious hybrids that died in a flood, are among us. They're just locked out of this physical realm and are

---

1. "Interlinear—1 Corinthians 9:27," Bible Hub.com, accessed November 22, 2024, https://biblehub.com/interlinear/1_corinthians/9-27.htm.

upset and very angry. They're going to be thrown in hell and incarcerated, but they are not yet. That's why, when Jesus addressed demons in people, they asked him not to send them to the pit, not to send them out of the area, not to torment them before their time (Matthew 8:29).

That gives us a clue of what's going on. These entities are trying to inhabit people. They want to stay in the same area that they were in before the flood. They did not get to be on Noah's ark. Only eight were righteous, perfect in their generations, it says, perfect in their genetics. Only eight of them out of the millions that died had not been corrupted.

These disembodied spirits do not have access to salvation. They have no way of getting back. They have not been judged yet. They are in a parallel realm beside us, and they hate us. But we are now accepted through Jesus Christ. The enemy that we deal with is rejected, and they project that rejection onto us. But actually, we're redeemed. Jesus died for every single person, even if they don't accept Him and go to hell.

> *Casting all your cares [all your anxieties, all your worries, and all your concerns, once and for all] on Him, for He cares about you [with deepest affection, and watches over you very carefully].*

> —1 Peter 5:7 AMP

The rejection that you go through in life causes anxiety. You feel that, and it is part of the curse. But you must reinforce what He did for you, and you have to know that He absolutely cares for you in the situations you're in. Don't let the devil lie about how God feels about you.

Therefore receive one another, just as Christ also received us, to the glory of God.

—Romans 15:7

The body is to welcome each other and make each other feel accepted. This is why Paul was so adamant about sin in the body because sin separates. People are selfish and sometimes do things on their own and don't consider the body. They make decisions that affect the group; then they have to be separated from the group. People that are operating in rejection cause a lot of damage, and they need deliverance. There is help for them. But if they don't accept it, if they don't operate in love toward each other, if they're selfish and self-exalting, then God will have to separate them from the rest of the group. This is how Paul and the apostles dealt with people in the church.

What then shall we say to these things? If God is for us, who can be against us?

—Romans 8:31

Anything that you encounter in this life that is contrary to the will of God and the Word of God is the enemy. You should make a separation and distinction. You do this by labeling the thief as the one who kills, steals, and destroys. You label Jesus Christ as being the One who gives you life and life more abundantly (John 10:10). Once you understand this, you can say, "If God is for me, who can be against me?"

Who shall separate us from the love of Christ? Shall tribulation, or distress, or persecution, or famine, or nakedness, or peril, or sword? As it is written:

*"For Your sake we are killed all day long; We are accounted
as sheep for the slaughter."*

*Yet in all these things we are more than conquerors
through Him who loved us. For I am persuaded that
neither death nor life, nor angels nor principalities nor
powers, nor things present nor things to come, nor height
nor depth, nor any other created thing, shall be able to
separate us from the love of God which is in Christ Jesus
our Lord.*

—Romans 8:35–39

As part of God's plan, Jesus was rejected so we could be free from
rejection. We are accepted by God. Matthew 13:54–58 says Jesus
came to His hometown and taught in the synagogue. While He was
there, they were astonished. They asked, "Where did this man get
all this wisdom and the ability to do these mighty works? Is he not
the carpenter's son?" They took offense at Him and rejected Him.
Then Jesus replied, "A prophet is not without honor, except in his
own hometown and in his own household." Jesus was not able to
do many works there because of their unbelief. Their unbelief hin-
dered Him because they had carnal knowledge of Him. He was their
family member, local to their town, but they did not discern he was
the Messiah. He was rejected by His own hometown because they
remembered Him as someone who had grown up there and viewed
him through that filter. So the ultimate enemy is rejection, but rejection works through unbelief.

You have been bought with a price, and God has restored you. You
will need to work through unbelief so that you can accept that truth.
You must allow God to win you over in these areas.

Appendix 1

Listening for His Still, Small Voice

I want to leave you with one more thought. During my heavenly visitation, one of the most important things that Jesus showed me was about the still, small voice. Besides the Word of God, this is the most prominent and important aspect of our Christian lives. The still, small voice of the Lord is how He leads us 90–95 percent of the time. When I used the word *voice*, it's not necessarily audible. It's more of a leading, a knowing, and a nudging.

As we've discussed, you can meditate on the Word of God. Then you pray, pray in the Spirit, building yourself up in your most holy faith, remaining in the love of God (Jude 1:20–21). This will give you balance, but then you will be led by God, like with an extremely soft, still voice.

I want to encourage you here. The Lord showed me that He leads us by lighting the candle of the Lord inside us. That small voice of the Lord, that whisper, is not always apparent. There is so much noise on this earth. I saw it when I came back. So many voices and the world, really, vie for our attention. The Lord showed me that the spirit of this world and the way it's set up here is designed to pull you away from Him, steal your attention, keep you busy, and create a lot of noise. So many voices try to grab your attention. Many demonic things are going on around you. These try to clutter the atmosphere to prohibit you from hearing that still, small voice.

Everything here is competing against God's voice, and you must be careful that you only give place to the Word of God and the Spirit of God. Those should have the highest priority in your life. Then, you must be careful not to feed yourself too much on other things that could cloud, corrupt, or make it more difficult to distinguish the voice of God. I believe that everyone hears God's voice. His voice is in every Christian. He is speaking to every one of us all the time, but we don't hear His voice because we think something spectacular should happen. However, the real supernatural way that God speaks to us is through this still, small voice.

This all means you must have time alone with Him. You must be quiet; don't expect it to be a certain way. You simply wait and let God speak to you. Give yourself at least fifteen minutes a day. If you want to be a minister, you will need a longer quiet time with the Lord: at least two hours. But start with fifteen minutes of sitting in quiet, meditating on the goodness of God, and giving Him your attention. Don't say anything. Just let God begin to renew that intimate relationship with you so that He can nudge you and you can respond.

Again, the still, small voice is not an actual voice that we would hear. It is that knowing and that communication when God will give you a nudge in a certain direction. You'll get a light: green, red, or yellow. Just use that image to get you started. Think of the green light as a go, that's a knowing, and a red light means to stop. The yellow light just means to proceed with caution. This will help you mature and begin to hear His voice in a more profound way.

Appendix 2

The Forty-First Floor

I recently had another dream that has greatly impacted me. I believe it is for the church as a whole and for you individually. In the dream, I was at the entrance of a very, very tall building that resembled a large hotel. It was forty feet wide and forty stories high. Jesus was there with me as I entered the building. Together, we got on the elevator and went all the way up to the fortieth floor.

We got out to an amazing sight. The whole floor was a beautiful living area. If I were to order a mansion in Heaven, this is what I would ask for. Everything was the way I liked it, and beautiful dark mahogany wood was everywhere. In the dream, this was Kathi's and my condominium. My whole staff was up there—nearly sixty people—and they were all standing around, fellowshipping.

As I stood there with Jesus, I saw someone I know, a man named David, who owns and operates a ranch in northern Texas. As he walked toward me, Jesus said, "Ask him how he goes on to his next phase."

Since I knew he had been a long-term success, I asked him, "What is the secret to your success over these forty years?"

He replied, "Well, the secret to going on with the Lord in the next phase, this final phase of ministry, is that there is another floor: the forty-first floor."

Forty is an important symbolic number. We see this number many times in the Bible: forty years in the desert and then the entry into the promised land. Jesus spent forty days in the desert, and on the forty-first day, He returned in power to His earthly ministry. The forty-first floor in the dream represents what is next.

After David spoke, another elevator door appeared right beside the elevator door we had just exited. As an elevator attendant stepped out and held the door, David said, "This goes to your office, and you're the only one allowed up there—just you and God. That's my secret: going to the forty-first floor, which is you and God. That is how you are going to finish your ministry—in that phase."

Then Jesus said, "You can get in the elevator."

I just want to encourage you that there will be closure to anything you're going through. There will be a graduation. There is a promotion after you go through your training phase.

Appendix 3

Be of Good Cheer

Recently, I had an encounter—a type of vision when I was with Jesus. He said to me, "I'm going to skip you past a lot of hardship that you're about to go through."

When I had this vision, everything seemed to be going fine. I saw a highway where a long line of people were standing. Jesus reached out His hand and grabbed my arm. Together, we accelerated past everyone. "Because you have submitted to the yoke of the Lord, allowed Me to discipline you, and have let Me teach you, I am going to put you a hundred days ahead."

He then placed me back in the line and added, "Your character is being formed by the walk you have with Me. Because you have been so submissive to that and have worked with Me and My Spirit, I am going to skip over these next one hundred days."

I replied, "Lord, I feel like this is cheating."

He responded, "Kevin, I can do whatever I want." Jesus then said goodbye to me and left.

Many of us are going through hardships—trials and tribulations. In John 16:33, Jesus said, "In the world you will have tribulation; but be of good cheer, I have overcome the world." This is how I felt when I was with Jesus. In that moment, He was my overcoming Creator who came to visit me. He explained that my character was being formed and that I was learning all the lessons I needed. He said He was going to skip over a lot of the trials and tribulations and put me ahead.

I want to encourage you that God can blindside you with a miracle—He can do whatever He wants!

Salvation Prayer

Lord God,

I confess that I am a sinner.

I confess that I need Your Son, Jesus.

Please forgive me in His Name.

Lord Jesus, I believe You died for me and that You

are alive and listening to me now.

I now turn from my sins and welcome

You into my heart. Come and take control of my life.

Make me the kind of person You want me to be.

Now, fill me with Your Holy Spirit,

who will show me how to live for You.

I acknowledge You before men

as my Savior and my Lord.

In Jesus's name. Amen.

IF YOU PRAYED THIS PRAYER,
PLEASE GET IN TOUCH WITH US AT

info@kevinzadai.com
for more information and material.

We welcome you to join our network at
warriornotes.tv for access to exclusive programming.

To enroll in our ministry school, go to:
www.warriornotesschool.com

Visit **www.kevinzadai.com** for
additional ministry materials.

About Dr. Kevin Zadai

Kevin Zadai, PhD, was called to the ministry at the age of ten. He attended Central Bible College in Springfield, Missouri, where he received a bachelor of arts in theology. Later, he received training in missions at Rhema Bible College, a ThD from Primus University, and a PhD from Life Christian University. Dr. Kevin L. Zadai is dedicated to training Christians to live and operate in two realms simultaneously—the supernatural and the natural.

At age thirty-one, Kevin met Jesus in Heaven, got a second chance at life, and received a revelation that he could not fail because it is all rigged in our favor! Kevin holds a commercial pilot license and is retired from Southwest Airlines after twenty-nine years as a flight attendant. He is the founder and president of Warrior Notes School of Ministry. He and his lovely wife, Kathi, reside in New Orleans.